Ladies' Abecedary

Arden Levine

Harbor Editions
Small Harbor Publishing

Ladies' Abecedary
Copyright © 2021 ARDEN LEVINE
All rights reserved.

Cover art by Rosemary Feit Covey
Cover design by Rico Frederick
Book layout by Allison Blevins and Hannah Martin

LADIES' ABECEDARY
ARDEN LEVINE
ISBN 978-1-7359090-5-9
Harbor Editions,
an imprint of Small Harbor Publishing

For Jacklyn, who taught me letters.

CONTENTS

There the whole question lies. Concede this little fulcrum and Archimedea will move the world before she has done with it; it becomes merely a question of time. Resistance must be made here or nowhere.

Thomas Wentworth Higginson
from "Ought Women to Learn the Alphabet?"
The Atlantic, February 1859

I don't fit into your dumb words.
Your alphabet is spelled with my blood.

Bikini Kill
from "Blood One"
1993

Ladies' Abecedary

A

fixes what hangs from women's bodies
in strands. She uses the *Diagnostic and Statistical Manual
(Fifth Edition)* and needle-nosed pliers.

Her women have mistaken glittering shrapnel
for gems. They fear losing them,
fear theft. So: Their bodies for safekeeping.

She twists silver wire and makes
tourniquets. The precious, paining segments
are then delicately removed.

B

, little she, was told she could be whoever she wished
in the school pageant. So she chose God.

> And God would wear a smudge
> of blue upon her face.

> And God would wear a gown
> of paper and language upon her body.

> And God would wear a crown
> of buoyant clouds upon her noggin.

> And in her throat, God
> would carry lightning, press it white and hard

> into attentive air, like teeth newly cut through tender gums.

In the audience, attendants remark on God:

So many times, God
pissed on me.

> *Often, God has thrown her hands wild,*
> *like warring starlings.*

> > *Twice, God briefly disappeared,*
> > *leaving me blind.*

> > > *Once, God vomited, exaltedly,*
> > > *into my cupped, supplicant hands.*

> > > *Amen.*

C & D

walk by, smell
like they've been
up
to
down
to
every-
thing
they're into.

Pressed together damp
flowers clamped
between layers between
hours
                          cool
                  looks
          kill
time.

Their legs are.

Their legs between
their heels
their hips are

their trapeze tightrope
trampoline.

Swingstretch, smack.

Say *oh*. They say

oh   *oh*

oh.

E

held, in beautiful unadorned hands,
a hardcover book.
She read it, regarded the room,
reflected. Patient.

The hardcover book
sat closed and attentive
reflected her, patient,
as he explained to her the procedure.

Sitting close and attentive,
the light above washed her pale
as he explained the procedure
and what it would be like after.

The light above washed her pale;
her hair fell around her face.
And what would it be like, after?
She rested the book on its spine.

Her hair fell around her face
as she removed her clothes;
she rested the book on its spine
creased and split to center.

She removed her clothes
and became part of the table.
Spine creased, she split to center,
forefingers touching like a circuit.

Once her spine was part of the table
he inserted rods in her to open her.
Her fingers, touching like a circuit,
resembled the thin metal rods.

As he inserted rods in her to open her
she started to bleed. A machine
with a sound resembling thin metal rods

clattered like coarse wind chimes.

She started to bleed into the machine,
which extracted a condition from her,
and a clatter like coarse wind chimes
sounded in her body cavity. Emptied,

her face a confusion of threads,
extracted from the table, a conditional object,
emptied of sound, her body an aching cavity,
she arose. She arranged her limbs.

She held herself, beautiful and unadorned.
Someone had closed the book, her page was lost.
He had left, the walls were quiet.
She read the textured walls, regarded the room.

F

opens a beer on the first Sunday
after Thanksgiving and tells everyone

about this year's pies, about how most of the customers
wanted cherry and not the usual pumpkin or apple,

and how orders flew in like insects through open windows.
Then she says that late Wednesday night she dropped a tray of eight,

watched them shatter their faces
against the kitchen tiles, spill their ruby innards.

What did you do then? everyone asks.
Roll dough. She places that reply so casually down

as if she had described knocking over a cup of water in her sleep
and waking to find the floor already near dry; this, and not a story

of toil in making, toil in cleaning, toil in remaking, mourning loss.
Anyway, she claims to have liked the second batch better:

smooth, clean edges. Full.

G

has a cabinet in Santa Fe that contains an anatomy.
Included here:

1.
Tiny bones,
micro-mementos mori, e.g.,
the radius that radiates light fingers.

2.
The paintbrush,
and the palette on which
the brush-tongue clicks.

3.
The paints, the skin of
unblended and unblemished
blue and blue.

H

still works at Poe's house, tends
to artifacts and ghosts.

The winter that the pipes cracked
a black fly was her only visitor.

She was not surprised when he
revealed himself: the deceased
always return in his stories.

Winged and wary, he could hear
the voices between the walls

and within them, confirm
the beloved dead
                        safe in her
                        keeping.

I

ran so hard, right out of the old *Gemeinschaft*.
U.S. soldiers liberated her
with Converse sneakers. She got
Levi's blue jeans, too, and wise
to how fast a girl can go

when the fabric wraps around both legs.
She ran so hard that she ran to America, so fast
that the consonants fell
out of her mouth, so she picked up
the ones she could reach and put them back

in new/other places. She got real
mouthy and handy, got all sorts
of paper and tenure, drove the Capitol Beltway
in a Ford, stopped running, stopped
walking, *halt*.

J

says, speaking of the hard-won
conclusions,   *it's good*

to know, no matter
how you have been treated or mis-
treated,   *what it is*
you deserve. Her kind of black:

high-balance credit cards
and high-heeled balancing acts,
cigarillos,   that voice

like sliding

the mourner's armband
up the sleeve. When she goes
to the other place,   her voice

is the cemetery drive in Cadillac
hearses.   She says

the other place and sometimes
the good place,   *ah yes.*

K

lived in a cold land atop a high mountain
in a house with a long staircase and nine sisters.
Every day, the sisters would descend the 25 steps
in height order (each neatly clicking her heels
on the 13th step), collect mittens warmed by the stone
hearth, and prepare for the journey into the snow.

Outside, the cold land had few intentions, the snow
had a body and an identity, and the mountain
was rarely a hard surface. Each one stone-
willed, supplied with mittens, the ten sisters
formed a line in height order out the door, heels
against the floor, snare-drumming tiny steps.

The sisters quietly hummed together as their steps
carried them one by one into the snow,
its body eating their small bodies head to heels,
biting down on and swallowing door, house, mountain,
cold land in the snow's mouth, digested around the sisters.
Yet the sisters had intentions, and they had the stones.

As tallest, she was the leader, and it was she who held the stones
in the bag, the others relying on her assured steps
and the stones' assured bodies. Here is how the sisters
would tell the story: The tall one drops a stone in the snow.
If the stone lands, there is cold land below, the mountain
has a body. If the stone does not land, *sisters, dig in your heels.*

So: Heels
if the stone
doesn't find the body of the mountain.
And: Steps
if the snow
covers solid cold land below the sisters.

All day, as they venture, the ten tall-to-short sisters
keep their tidy line of ten bodies, each set of left heels
landing, then right, in the devouring mouth of snow,

mittened, blinded, humming, kept safe by the stones
from the soft edge of the cold land, their tiny steps
touching only where there existed a surface to the mountain.

When they return from the snow, they hang the bag of stones
near the hearth, the sisters' mittens carefully hung, heels
aching from so many steps, eyes to the window, the mountain.

L

claims to him that she's not the type
to drape herself in serpents and offer
curious apples, but isn't that just
the lie such a woman would tell?

Someone wants a bite. She mentions

that in the photo at the farm, her arms
embrace a goat with a fetish for her hair
so she tied it up, but it kept trying.
No way to sate a satyr.

Sounds like a horny goat. He feels

a tiny cartoon beast lean
on his neck, tap a pitchfork against
his clavicle. Before long, that tail will slip
halfway down his throat. *Come here, come.*

M

, a widowed scientist, handled volatile matter
with her married lover, suffered
from exposure to toxicity.

As they discovered and were discovered,
Le Journal wrote of *the fires of radium*
which beam, which burn.

N

receives gifts from them, broken
just for her: Here is

a bright patch of red
on a blue quilt. Here are
thick, smooth splinters and
glittering shale chipped
from the leveled mountain.

Here, they brought her
the last zinnia and some water
to hold it for a day or two.
After that, she will
hang it by its heels
so blood rushes to its head.

(The water is no good
for drinking or washing
or making tea.)

Here is a whistle
that sounds
at an inaudible frequency
and a piano with its strings cut.

They bring her
here: low. And yet here:
her raised, accepting arms,
her empty, upturned palms.

O

lifted a millipede from the dirt, shook it
in her small hands. In fear, it excreted the sweet scent
of cyanide: the carbon-nitrogen almond.

Evolution is not always perfect. A protective substance
that does not explicitly state *I am death in the mouth*
will at best confuse, at worst invite.

P

can't have any part of her
body touching any other
part of her body. It's hard

for more reasons that you'd expect.
She carries napkins everywhere
(no licking of fingers). Sleeping (even

alone) requires unconscious agility
and unseemly blanket arrangement.
Just imagine: No folding hands. No

crossing legs. (No flummoxed
striking of head with palm, even.)
No bringing knees up to

shoulders during or bringing elbows
down to knees after. The whole
surface irritant and irritator, she

holds her poses hard, prays against
accidental contact, daydreams of
taking herself into her own arms

and swaying, swaying.

Q

was never like, *hey, a shoe sounds like my kinda digs,* but when your credit sucks and rents are lousy at some point you say: *any port in the storm,* or maybe *any galosh, by gosh,* which she actually does say and it always gets laughs, y'know, the joint is a goddamn trick: those tight laces, that shiny leather, the slide down the tongue that takes you down inside . . . fuck, that tongue is an escalator! and the gents, they all come by to *play knick-knack on my gate* 'cause if you can light a match against the sole you'll see there's a back door, come on 'round, likker in the toes and poker down at heel, if he gets at her good he may add one more brat to the brood, but she'll tear out the teeth in the mouth that tells that for-shit story to her face: *I never spanked them once, not soundly or softly, my babies are all beauties in booties.*

R

had a dream: the baby was coming
much too soon. On hands and knees
thinking nothing

would survive this, she also thought: if this
were the last moment, how could she
part from her life and leave behind

her books?   Her waking self thinks: Strange
to be less concerned with dying and never
meeting her child. She pulls a book off the shelf,

reads aloud the words *water, fear,* and *almost*
when they appear, words agitating
for attention, wailing and terrified, *God help me.*

S

sees cake, but nothing she wants to eat will fit in her mouth.
There's a pretty dress, but her mouth is a frayed hemline.
There's a durable pair of wings, but she won't wear them.

It's a soft spring day, and the dress can be a silken armor.
These are fine walls, and they race each other to the ceiling.
The drumbeats are distant and she feels them under her tongue.

There's a pair of wings that someone stole and gave to her.
The drumbeats are approaching and her teeth ache.
It's an edible autumn day, but she won't bite down.

This is a fine chair, and its legs race each other to the floor.
It's a mild winter day and her tongue is pinned under the chair.
This is a pretty dress and it can be a silken tourniquet.

T

is the one in all the songs:
passenger seat,
map on her thighs, toes dashing   St. Christopher.

There is some place he took her from,   or some place
she left with him, perhaps
they were tossed out

of the sky, lost their lease on God.   So, *El Camino*
the drive, the unruly asphalt gardens,
the tailpipe fumes

like a long exhale, the tapering
of their history. They stop
only when there is no money   or no gas,

or for her to wash his jeans, bent over
roadside rivers,
the soft flesh of her feet on stones.   So long nowhere,

they've all forgotten her name (except   for him),
so sometimes she is *T*_____,
and sometimes __*t*_____

and sometimes _____.   Until the day
she kneels in San Miguel and prays
for a little girl,

a small house, a patch of land, and   the tune
turns from their engine's southerly strum

to the percussion   of her two heels,

northward,   at a breakaway run.

U

had made two wrong assumptions:

1) that you could find the missing,
   either with maps or with technology.

2) that words would keep you safe.

V

positioned herself above the tree line
and played the acrid voice of a screech owl on a tape player
to rouse the birds. Then she worried

that she had corrupted their confidence
in daylight, made real their fears
of morning deaths by evening executioners.

Later, she slept beneath nightmare views
of tall buildings grown downward from clouds
like steel stalactites, residents with unevolved wings

crawling out of windows, descending
toward the roof, an upending of her notions
of knowledge and mercy.

W & X

thirst for each other. They drink

tenderly from seashell eyelids,
deeply from hollows between ribs.

They drink from palms like slaking wells,
from the bodies' lush, draining clouds,

and their woodwind voices flood,
riverbank arteries rush, basin eyes brim.

They pour each other's muscles down
their throats, swallow the unblossomed

orchid shapes of shoulders. They drink
with lips and tongues like shorelines

defined by the arrival of the tide.

Y

talks about fluid breathing,

> how she has aligned the motion

of arms and neck and mouth

> to manage the human need

for oxygen. She was born

> with webbed fingers that catch handfuls

of current and pull her through.

> She: one more wave.

She waves. She comes

> back slick and glinting, flicks

her toes. She runs again

> into open water, and her gait

slows not from contact with water

> but because she has arrived.

Z

sleeps in a chrysalis curve
and dreams

of a long hibernation
during which her bones

will be re-set into
shapes resembling wings.

ACKNOWLEDGMENTS

I am grateful to those who produce the following publications, where many of the poem-ladies (or earlier versions of them) made their debuts:

"A": *Washington Square Review* (as "Healer")

"B": *Indiana Review* (as "Little she")

"E": *SWWIM* (as "Pantoum [Procedure]")

"F", "G", "H", "I", and "M": *Cagibi* (as "The First Sunday After Thanksgiving", and "[In Santa Fe:], [In Philadelphia:], [In Berlin:], [In: Paris]"). Note: "M" includes a variation on a line from an article in the Paris newspaper *Le Journal*, November 4, 1911.

"J" and "L": *Barrow Street* (as "Some Measure of Comfort" and "On One Shoulder")

"K": *Zone 3* (as "The tall one")

"N": *The Lifted Brow* (as "Gifts")

"O": *Bone Bouquet* (as "The last time on this trail")

"P" and "S": *Cream City Review* (as "The poor thing" and "The birthday girl")

"R": *Rogue Agent* (as "Bearing")

"T": *Epiphany Magazine* (as "Far Gone")

"V": *Free State Review* (as "Observation Inversion")

I am also grateful for the support and love of my family and partner, the encouragement and joy of steadfast friends, the forbearance and enthusiasm of colleagues in social service and public service, the passion and perspective of those we serve, and the wise guidance of numerous readers, editors, and educators. You are present in these stories and in more yet to be told.

Arden Levine's poems have appeared in *Harvard Review, RHINO, River Styx, Sycamore Review, Sixth Finch,* and other journals, and have been featured in *AGNI Online, The Missouri Review*'s Poem-of-the-Week, WNYC's *Radiolab,* and *American Life in Poetry* (selected by former U.S. Poet Laureate Ted Kooser). Arden currently serves as a Foundation Board Member for *Beloit Poetry Journal* and previously served as an Assistant Editor at *Epiphany Magazine.* She lives in New York City, where her daily work focuses on housing affordability, homelessness prevention, and equitable community development.

CPSIA information can be obtained
at www.ICGtesting.com
Printed in the USA
LVHW042009261122
734083LV00005B/604